" LEARN TO LOVE

OUR PLANET "

This is planet **Earth**.

Planet Earth is enormous!

There are
almost **8 billion**
people living on it.

Planet **Earth** is very kind to us.
It creates a human life and
other living organisms and creatures
like plants and animals.
It also provides us with things such as:
-air to breath
-water to drink
-food to eat
-a place to live
All those things are essential
for us to survive on planet Earth
which is our home planet.

Take a look around you and
appreciate things
that surrounds us:
lands, seas, oceans,
mountains, forests,
desserts. Diversity of
plants, animals, and much more
are all part of our
beautiful nature on planet Earth
which gives us comfortable
and happy life's.

The Earth knows
how to take
care of us
so we should
do the same
for Earth.

What happens
if we don't take care
of our planet Earth?

If we don't take care of our planet Earth we will eventually be unable to: breath clean air drink clean water eat food that is not poisoned and there will be floods.

Our planet will be polluted with rubbish and other toxic things.

So HERE are the steps we need to take to help our planet Earth .

Its called **3 Rs Rule:**
Reduce, Reuse, Recycle.

REDUCE –meaning use less of

PLASTIC: is not biodegradable and is harmful for the nature, humans and animals. **Reducing** helps protect environment, saves energy and prevents pollution. Plastic straws, plastic bags, plastic bottles can be replaced with paper straws fabric bags and reusable drink bottles.

WATER: remember to turn off the tap when you brush your teeth. Take showers instead of baths. This will help to preserve our environment and it will **reduce** the energy required to process and deliver it to homes, schools, farms and other places.

ENERGY AND ELECTRICITY:
Turn off the radio and tv when
you finish listening and watching.
Turn off the lights when you
leave the room and heating
when you leave your house.
This will protect the air
that we, breathe and it will
save your money.

DRIVE LESS IN THE CAR
This will save our planet from
creating pollutions and will help
to save our air and
breath in less toxics.
If we use cars more often the
atmosphere will heat up.
Arctic ice will start melting
and the water levels in
the oceans will rise,
and small countries and islands
will slowly be flooded or
washed away.

REUSE-meaning use more then once

If we don't need something we
can give it away or sell it
instead of throwing it away.
This will help reduce energy,
air, water and other materials.

Things we can **REUSE:**

Toys

Books

Clothes

Sport equipment

Furniture
and many
other things

RECYCLE- meaning turn used items into new items

And give a new life to things that you don't need anymore. **Recycling** saves energy prevents pollution and reduces landfills.

Items we can RECYCLE:

glass (food containers bottles, jars)
cardboard (cereal, snack boxes and other clean boxes)
paper (magazines, newspaper, letters)
plastic (bottles and containers (found in your house)
metals (tins, steel cans, aluminium)

Ask your parents to help you put those items into separate bins and then take them to **recycle point** in your town and put them into special departments for plastic, paper, metal etc. They will be converted to new things and used over and over again.

PAPER

PLASTIC

OTHER THINGS YOU CAN RECYCLE:
- wood
- batteries
- garden waist
- iron and steel

MORE WAYS to help carrying for our planet
Get involved and inspire others
by taking parts in projects like
"Save the planet" "Earth's Day"
"Recycling Parade "" and help
cleaning places like
parks and beaches.
Spread the message and
invite others to be part of it.

WE ARE THE PLANET

LOVE OUR PLANET

SAVE PLANET EARTH

CHARITY SHOP

BUY RECYCLED
Things like:
clothes
-toys
books
household goods.

LIBRARY
Instead of buying new books you can borrow them from a Library and buy only your favourite books.

REMEMBER to always throw the rubbish to the bins. Littering could be harmful to our, our animals and plants lives. It can cause harmful germs and bacteria that could make us sick. It could even cause fires.

PAPER

GROW YOUR OWN
foods like fruits, vegetables herbs, plants or even a tree. Eating these foods will improve your health as they are organic (clear from chemicals) It will also help wildlife and it will save you money.

HERBS

MAKE A PROMISE

" I will do my best to keep
"**3Rs rule**"
Reduce, Reuse, Recycle!
Save the energy around me
and use less of everything.
I will take part and learn
about how to take care of our
planet and make it a better
place to live.
I will spread the message and
inspire others to
be part of it.
Now I'm "Save our planet
Earth" on a mission kid" !

Thank you to my gorgeous daughter Juliette
for inspiring me to write this book! x

Made in the USA
Las Vegas, NV
17 February 2022